The Alien Code: Unlocking the Matrix

Jessie Contreras

Published by Summon UFOs, 2024.

THE ALIEN CODE: UNLOCKING THE MATRIX

First edition. September 13, 2024.

ISBN: 979-8224143177

Written by Jessie Contreras.

Table of Contents

To the seekers of the skies and the explorers of consciousness—

This book is dedicated to those who look beyond the ordinary and feel the quiet pull of something greater calling from the stars. To the ones who dare to question, to reach, and to make contact not only with the unknown, but with the deeper parts of themselves.

May your intention be clear, your mind be open, and your signal be strong.

Chapter 1: Awakening from the Matrix

1.1 The First Glimpse of Reality

Recognizing the signs that life may be more than what it seems often begins as a whisper, a fleeting thought that dances at the edges of our consciousness. It can feel like a gentle tug at our reality, urging us to question the mundane aspects of our existence. I can still remember that moment when the routine chatter of everyday life began to fade, replaced by an underlying frequency, a subtle vibration. It happened in the most ordinary of places—a coffee shop, surrounded by people lost in their screens. As I gazed out the window, I noticed how truly disconnected we all seemed, ensnared by our own realities. The coffee, the chatter, the hurried pace of life felt scripted, almost artificial. It was in that moment I realized: could there be more beyond what I perceived? This glimmer of awareness was the first step toward awakening. It wasn't just a thought; it was a call to dive deeper, to peel back the layers that shrouded what I began to suspect was a more profound existence than the one I was living.

When you start to recognize these signs and follow your curiosity, pay attention to the signs around you. Take a moment to observe the night sky and allow yourself to wonder about the vastness of the universe. Engage in mindful practices like meditation, as they can help open your mind and heart to experiences that lie just beyond the surface of daily life. Even keeping a journal of your dreams can serve as a powerful tool to unlock insights into the nature of reality. These simple actions can lead you down a path of discovery, where the first glimpse of reality can transform into a profound understanding of who you are and what your connection is to the expansive universe around you.

1.2 Breaking the Chains of Illusion

We grow up in a world filled with expectations and norms that shape the way we see ourselves and our realities. From a young age, I felt the weight of societal conditioning pressing on my shoulders, dictating how I should act, what I should believe, and even whom I should associate with. It wasn't until I stepped back and began to question these beliefs that I realized how much they limited my perception and stifled my freedom. Like many of us, I was taught to accept the world as it is, rather than explore what it could be. Breaking free from these invisible chains requires deep introspection, an honest re-evaluation of what I had accepted as truth. I had to challenge my own inner dialogue and ask myself, "Whose beliefs am I living by?" By recognizing the narratives imposed on me, I found the strength to let go of the limiting beliefs that had kept me confined. Finding out that the only limits that truly exist are those I allow is where my journey to freedom began.

One night, after weeks of wrestling with these ideas, I met someone who would forever change my perspective. They shared their story of how they had once been trapped in a corporate job, bound to the grind of 9-to-5, feeling suffocated by expectations. Despite facing immense challenges, they eventually took the leap into the unknown, pursuing their passion for art and creativity. Their journey was filled with uncertainties, but the joy of living authentically brought profound fulfillment, serving as a guiding light for others. Hearing their story reminded me that resilience often blooms in the most unexpected places. Empowerment lies not just in overcoming external obstacles but in dismantling the internal barriers we erect. When we choose to reclaim our narrative, we open the door for countless others. Such stories become beacons of hope, encouraging each of us to break free from our own cages of conformity.

The lessons learned from my experiences and those of others are invaluable. It's essential to challenge the status quo and recognize that perceptions can be shifted. One practical tip that helped me immensely was to create a daily practice of mindfulness and reflection. Taking a moment to sit in silence, observing my thoughts without judgment, allowed me to discover the roots of my conditioning. This practice helped me identify the stories I had been told and understand how they no longer served me. By finding clarity in stillness, I was able to see beyond the illusion and summon the courage to rewrite my story. Accepting this journey can lead to the most transformative experiences, unveiling the freedom we all seek.

1.3 The Call to Adventure

The hero's journey is more than just an archetypal tale; it's a reflection of our own lives. Each of us can relate to the call to adventure. It's that moment when we realize we crave something beyond our everyday routine. For some, it may start as a flicker of curiosity, a yearning to explore hidden possibilities. I remember feeling it for the first time when I looked up at the night sky, wondering if there was more to this reality than what I could see. This quest is about forging our paths, confronting challenges, and discovering parts of ourselves we never knew existed.

Embracing the unknown is essential in this journey. Diving into uncertainty can be daunting, yet it often leads to deeper truths about our existence and reality itself. The universe does not lay out a detailed map for those who seek answers; instead, it offers an invitation to wander. When I first started seeking interactions with UFOs, I had to confront my fears and step beyond what was familiar. Each encounter became a lesson, a step towards unraveling the complex tapestry of existence. The magic happens when we surrender to this unknown, allowing the cosmos to guide us towards understanding our place within it.

To truly embrace this call, we must learn to let go of our rigid perceptions. Open-mindedness can be our strongest asset as we navigate this mysterious journey. Standing on the brink of what we think we know, remember to take the leap into the extraordinary. If you're yearning for meaningful experiences or wish to summon UFOs, start by challenging your own beliefs and perceptions of reality. It may be as simple as stargazing with intent, actively seeking connections with the unseen, or quietly listening to the whispers of the universe. Each moment spent exploring the unknown can bring you closer to your own adventure.

Chapter 2: Understanding the Matrix

2.1 The Nature of Reality

As I delve deeper into the nature of reality, I find myself exploring philosophical concepts and theories that challenge my very perception of existence. Philosophers like Descartes and Kant have long pondered what is real and what is illusion. Descartes famously stated, I think, therefore I am, which implies that our consciousness is fundamental to our understanding of reality. This relationship between thought and existence has intrigued me, creating a bridge to the deeper mysteries of life and, perhaps, the universe itself. Kant argued that our experiences are filtered through our senses and that what we perceive is not necessarily the truth. This idea resonates with me, particularly when I consider how easily our perceptions can be manipulated. It raises questions about the true nature of reality—are we perceiving a fabricated world, a constructed matrix, or part of an expansive cosmic truth? The connection to UFOs and the idea of extraterrestrial life adds layers to this exploration. If there are beings out there beyond our understanding, what does that say about the limitations of our perceptions?

Personal beliefs play a crucial role in shaping how we interpret existential truths. Throughout my journey, I have realized that my understanding of reality is influenced by my experiences and the beliefs I hold dear. Each encounter, whether with nature, other people, or even those spontaneous moments of synchronicity, contributes to this tapestry of understanding. Reflecting on my own experiences, I can see how personal beliefs lead us to see or disregard truths that may be right in front of us. For instance, the belief that we are part of something greater nudges me to look toward the skies with wonder and hope. It connects me to the potential for contact with extraterrestrial life, pushing me to engage with the cosmos in a more profound way. The notion that my consciousness can influence the reality I experience encourages me to take active steps toward exploring these uncharted territories. This personal interpretation shapes my understanding of existence; it becomes a journey, one where we can expand our reality and maybe even learn to summon or connect with UFOs.

Being inquisitive about the nature of reality often leads to revelations that go beyond traditional thinking. Engaging with the idea of reality as a construct opens doors to possibilities. As I stand under the vast night sky, embracing the mystery of what lies beyond, I remind myself that exploring consciousness and shifting perceptions can lead to powerful insights. We can practice mindfulness and meditation to sharpen our awareness and cultivate a deeper understanding of ourselves and the universe. By doing so, we may unlock pathways to altered states of consciousness, enhancing our ability to connect with realms beyond our own. Perhaps it all starts with a simple intention—a heartfelt wish to connect with the unknown, to summon something extraterrestrial, to break free from the confines of the matrix that surrounds us.

2.2 The History of Human Perception

Tracing the evolution of human thought and perception through different cultures and epochs reveals a fascinating journey. From ancient civilizations that looked to the stars for guidance to modern thinkers questioning the very nature of reality, our understanding has always been shaped by the times we live in. Ancient Egyptians viewed the cosmos through a lens steeped in mythology, interpreting the movements of celestial bodies as divine messages. As we move through history, the Greeks introduced logic and reason, laying the groundwork for scientific inquiry that still influences us today. The Renaissance brought a renewed curiosity about the natural world, inspiring a shift from superstition to observation. Each culture and epoch contributed unique insights that have shaped our collective perception, evolving from spiritual interpretations to a more empirical understanding of existence.

Reflecting on how historical events shape modern perspectives on reality is essential for grasping why we perceive the world as we do. The Age of Enlightenment sparked a revolution in thought, challenging long-held beliefs and leading to unprecedented advancements in science and philosophy. This shift caused many to rethink the nature of existence, encouraging a focus on individual experience and empirical evidence. In more recent times, the social upheavals of the 20th century - from wars to technological revolutions - have further diversified our perspectives. Nowadays, we find ourselves at a crossroads. With technology influencing how we perceive information, the digital age has created a new reality for many, challenging our understanding of authenticity. As we navigate this space, it's crucial to remember that our perceptions are shaped not just by what we see, but by the history behind our eyes, and the events that have etched themselves into our collective psyche.

Engaging with this knowledge encourages us to critically examine our perception of reality. One practical way to deepen this understanding is to reflect on the narratives that have shaped your beliefs. Consider the historical context of those narratives and how they may influence your perception today. By acknowledging these influences, we can start to peel back the layers of our reality, opening the door to new possibilities. Embracing this journey not only aids in escaping the proverbial matrix but also facilitates a connection with the wider universe, possibly even opening doors to experiences like summoning UFOs, as our perceptions expand beyond conventional boundaries.

2.3 Modern-Day Matrix: Technology and Control

Technology has fundamentally changed the way we perceive and interact with the world around us. Every day, we find ourselves filtered through layers of screens and devices, each one altering our consciousness in subtle ways. For instance, social media platforms curate our feeds to show us content that resonates with our established beliefs, creating an echo chamber that can distort our understanding of reality. As I scroll through my phone, I often wonder how many hours I've unintentionally wasted absorbing information that confirms what I already think, rather than challenging it. The digital landscape constantly begs for our attention, shaping our perceptions of what is important and diverting our focus from the tangible world. This pervasive influence has morphed our relationship with reality, making it easy to forget the richness of in-person experiences and deeper human connections.

Finding the balance between embracing technology and becoming overly dependent on it has become a vital skill. While it offers incredible convenience and access to knowledge, it's crucial to recognize when it starts to overwhelm our lives. I've seen how detaching occasionally can lead to profound clarity. Taking breaks from devices allows me to reconnect with my surroundings and reflect on my thoughts without constant interference. During these moments of silence, I've found new insights and creative solutions that technology sometimes clouds. Embracing technology should enhance our lives rather than dictate them; we must intentionally choose when to unplug and engage with the world authentically. To cultivate this balance, establishing tech-free zones in our homes or scheduled tech detoxes could be beneficial strategies to reclaim our focus and strengthen our mental well-being.

In this modern matrix where technology intertwines with our consciousness, it's essential to approach innovations with a mindful perspective. Recognizing the subtle ways technology shapes our thoughts and behaviors can empower us to make deliberate choices about what influences our lives. Engaging in practices like meditation or journaling helps me cut through the noise, fostering a personal sense of peace amid the chaos. Remember, while technology offers us the ability to navigate the universe creatively, maintaining a conscious relationship with it is key. Try to identify moments where you can step back, look up from your screen, and reconnect with the world around you; you may be surprised by the new dimensions of reality that unfold.

Chapter 3: The Language of the Universe

3.1 Frequencies and Vibrations

The universe is an intricate web where everything operates on frequencies. Everything – from the smallest particle to the largest galaxy – vibrates with a certain energetic frequency. I often find myself captivated by the idea that our thoughts and emotions are not just abstract feelings but also vibrations that affect the world around us. This interconnectedness is palpable in experiences where music or natural sounds seem to resonate with my very core. It stirs something deep within, reminding me that I am part of a grand mosaic of energies swirling around us. While many people live their lives unaware of these subtle frequencies, there lies a profound opportunity to tap into them. By becoming attuned to the vibrations within and around us, we can access a deeper understanding of the universe and our place within it.

My personal adventures into the realm of sound and vibrational healing have been eye-opening. I remember my first experience with a sound bath. As I lay there, the resonance of crystal bowls enveloped me, sending ripples of energy through my body. Each note awakened different feelings as I could almost visualize the vibrations dancing across the room. This wasn't just a path to relaxation; it felt like a deeper, spiritual cleansing. I emerged from that session with clarity and newfound energy, as if the sound had realigned my being. On another occasion, I attended a workshop focused on drum circles. The heartbeat of the drums connected us in a way that transcended spoken language. In that circle, it was clear that the rhythms propelled us into a space of unity and healing. These experiences convinced me that sound waves are not just pleasing to the ear but are potent tools for transformation.

Understanding how to harness these frequencies opens doors to new possibilities. Engaging with sound can be a gateway to summon experiences beyond our typical reality. Each of us has the power to tap into this collective energy; it just takes practice and awareness. Consider experimenting with different sounds in your environment. Play with audiovisual modalities or instruments that resonate with you. Simply find a quiet space, tune into your breath, and allow the natural sounds around you to guide you deeper into your own experience of vibration and frequency. The journey into understanding the language of the universe through sound can lead to profound insights and possibly even encounters that bridge our world with others beyond.

3.2 The Power of Intention

When I first started to delve into the idea of intention, it felt almost magical. I learned that focused intention could shape not just my thoughts but also the reality I experienced. It's like tuning a radio; when you set your intention clearly, you begin to hear the frequency that resonates with those goals and desires. This ability to create from thought is a concept woven deeply into the fabric of our existence. I remember a time when I was struggling with a decision. Instead of letting uncertainty cloud my mind, I sat quietly, closed my eyes, and visualized my desired outcomes. As I focused on those intentions, an overwhelming sense of clarity washed over me. Aligning my thoughts with specific intentions seemed to almost bend reality, transforming my path ahead.

Real-life examples of intention shaping outcomes intrigue me endlessly. There was a moment in my life when I first attempted to summon UFOs, grounded in a belief that intention could reach beyond the physical. I gathered a small group of friends with the same curiosity, and we went to a remote location under a starry sky. Before we began, we each shared our intentions, visualizing an otherworldly encounter. As we concentrated on our shared goals, the atmosphere shifted. Clouds parted, and suddenly, there appeared a bright light that danced across the sky in ways we had never seen before. It wasn't just coincidence; it felt like our intentions connected us to something greater. This experience illustrated how intention isn't merely an abstract concept; it manifests in our realities, opening doors to unimaginable experiences. The universe seemed to respond to our collective focus, reinforcing the idea that intention holds tremendous power over our lives.

The real treasure lies in learning how to harness this power daily. Creating a ritual can help solidify your intentions. Start by setting aside a few quiet moments each day to reflect on what you want to manifest. Whether it's a peaceful state of mind or an extraordinary experience, articulate it clearly. Write it down, visualize it, or even speak it out loud as if you're communicating with the universe itself. The key is consistent focus. When you align your energy with your intentions, the possibilities expand. Remember, every thought is a seed, and with nurturing, it has the potential to sprout into reality.

3.3 Cosmic Communication: Understanding Symbols

Identifying universal symbols can feel like tapping into a secret language of the cosmos. I discovered that certain shapes, colors, and even numbers possess meanings that span time and cultures. For instance, the spiral is a powerful symbol representing growth and evolution. When I began to notice spirals appearing everywhere—on shells, in the clouds, and even in art—I felt a connection to something greater than myself. This newfound awareness allowed me to communicate with the universe in a profound way. I realized that the stars and planets might be reaching out, whispering their messages through these symbols. Understanding these universal symbols can lead to a richer, more connected experience with the universe. It is as if they are invitations to explore the mysteries of existence. By becoming fluent in this cosmic language, we can unlock pathways to experiences that are beyond ordinary perception.

As I delved deeper into this exploration of symbols, my dreams became a fascinating tapestry of signs and messages. Dream symbols played a pivotal role in my personal journey of cosmic communication. I vividly remember one night when I dreamt of a large, glowing orb hovering above me. When I woke up, I felt an indescribable sense of peace. This orb later became a recurring motif in my dreams, and it felt like a friendly presence inviting me to engage more deeply with my spiritual quest. I began to jot down my dreams every morning and explore what each symbol meant to me. For instance, water often represented emotions and intuition, while flights often signified a desire for freedom. These insights allowed me to connect with my inner self and the universe at large. Sharing my experiences with friends opened up new discussions about the symbols they encountered in their own dreams, creating a community of cosmic explorers. It became clear that the universe is sending us signs—if only we take the time to listen and interpret them.

In practice, keeping a dream journal is immensely helpful. It not only helps in decoding messages from the universe but also strengthens your intuition. When dreams present symbols, take a moment to reflect on what those images signify for you personally. Sometimes the true meaning might not be apparent right away, so give it time. Another useful technique is to meditate on your experiences and visualize the symbols. Imagine them radiating messages that resonate with your intentions. Connecting with the cosmos is an ongoing journey, woven together by symbols and signs. Embrace them, share your insights, and remain open to the wonders that may come your way.

Chapter 4: Initiating Contact with UFOs

4.1 The Signs and Signals

Learning to recognize the signs that may indicate alien presence or interest requires an open mind and a willingness to observe the world from a different perspective. I began my journey by tuning into the subtle shifts in my environment. Strange lights flickering in the night sky, odd formations of clouds, or even the briefest sound that seems out of place can all serve as indicators. The energy in the air sometimes shifts, creating a palpable tension, almost electric. On evenings filled with profound stillness, I found it easier to pick up on these nuances. Birds suddenly stopping their chirping, or a group of animals falling silent, felt significant, as though nature itself reacted to something beyond our understanding. The tiniest instinct should be given attention; our intuition might be picking up on signals we can't readily see. Recognizing these signs isn't just about watching; it's about feeling and connecting deeply with our surroundings.

Describing momentary experiences that felt like potential contact moments is both exhilarating and surreal. I recall one specific night when the air was crisp and a perfect blanket of stars blanketed the sky. As I lay on the grass, staring upward, a sense of anticipation washed over me. Suddenly, without warning, a flash of light darted across the horizon. It was quick but surreal, piquing my curiosity. In that fleeting moment, I sensed an overwhelming presence, almost as if the universe held its breath, waiting for me to acknowledge it. On another occasion, while walking alone in a desolate area, I felt an inexplicable urge to look up. To my amazement, a triangular-shaped craft glided silently overhead, hidden behind the cloak of night. The only sound was my heart racing, and I couldn't shake the feeling that it was aware of me as much as I was aware of it. Each experience left me buzzing with questions and visions, fueling my desire to understand and connect further.

Being open to these signs and moments can enhance our ability to attract UFOs or initiate contact. Practice mindfulness and trust your intuition; the more you engage with the cosmos through meditation and observation, the more you'll begin to notice those elusive signals. Documenting your experiences can also help clarify patterns or connections over time. Take notes of your feelings, the environment, and any signs you observe; this will create a personal guidebook of sorts, strengthening your sensitivity to the unseen. Engaging with the universe is about creating a dialogue, and every small sign brings you one step closer to understanding the larger picture.

4.2 Preparing Your Mind and Space

Establishing a space where I can not only invite higher beings but also feel their presence requires careful thought and intention. I learned that the energy of my surroundings plays a significant role in how receptive I am during such encounters. To create the right environment, I begin by decluttering both my physical space and my mind. A clean, open area allows my thoughts to flow freely and diminishes distractions that could break my focus.

I often incorporate elements that resonate with me deeply. This could be calming music, fragrant incense, or even crystals that I feel drawn to. Each object serves as a conduit for higher vibrational energies, signaling to the universe my readiness to connect. Natural light is another essential element; I make it a point to spend time near a window or even outdoors, where the energy of nature amplifies my intentions. As I sit in this charged environment, I visualize a soft, inviting light surrounding me, welcoming those beings who wish to communicate.

An essential part of this journey is transforming my mindset. I have come to understand that belief plays a powerful role in shaping my experiences. I consciously choose to adopt an open perspective, allowing for the possibility that UFOs and extraterrestrial beings exist and are eager to connect. This shift often requires overcoming fear and skepticism, which can block the very channels I want to open. I remind myself that fear is a learned response and that by embracing curiosity instead, I can foster a more harmonious dialogue.

Another critical mindset shift involves letting go of the need for validation from others. I recognize that my experiences are valid, even if they differ from general perceptions. This realization empowers me to trust my intuition, allowing me to perceive events and signs that may go unnoticed by others. Meditation has been a transformative practice for me; it helps to quiet my mind and tune into the subtle energies around me. Whenever I feel anxious or doubtful, I return to my breath, anchoring myself in the present moment, and reaffirming my intentions to connect. Trusting myself and my intuition feels like unlocking a door to new possibilities.

By consciously curating my environment and mindset, I find that I am not only preparing for contact but also opening myself up to a richer experience of life itself. Engaging in practices like visualization can be incredibly powerful. I often visualize the beings I wish to connect with and imagine our communication flowing effortlessly, aligning my intentions with love and respect. The next time you sit down to summon a UFO or engage with higher beings, take a moment to assess your space and mindset; this preparation can significantly enhance your experience.

4.3 My First Encounter: A Personal Account

It was a clear night when I first encountered something I couldn't explain. I was standing on a hillside, far away from the city lights, gazing at the vastness of the star-studded sky. Suddenly, a bright light appeared above the tree line, darting back and forth in a way that was unlike any aircraft I had seen. The way it moved was fluid, almost playful, defying all logic I knew of physics. My heart raced as the light swelled in intensity, illuminating the landscape around me. I felt drawn to it, as if a silent call was being whispered to my very soul. Within moments, it hovered directly above me. The feeling of awe washed over me, mixed with a subtle fear—I was witnessing something beyond the ordinary.

This experience was transformative. Questions surged through my mind in the aftermath. What did I just see? Was it a spaceship, an alien presence, or simply an optical illusion? Yet, in the depths of my confusion, clarity began to emerge. I felt a profound sense of connection to the cosmos, as if I was part of a larger tapestry woven through time and space. The encounter opened a door to possibilities I had never considered before. It shattered my conventional understanding of reality and nudged me towards a more expansive mindset. This experience led me to explore how to summon such encounters deliberately, driving me into the world of intention and awareness.

In the weeks that followed, I found myself more attuned to the universe and its subtleties. I began meditating under the stars, calling upon the energies of the cosmos with an open heart and curious spirit. Each time I stepped outside, I felt a gentle anticipation, as if the universe was listening and ready to respond. This evolved into a personal practice—a way to not just seek and summon, but to understand. The key lies in setting your intention. When you connect with a genuine desire for knowledge, that openness attracts experiences beyond the ordinary. So if you're yearning to break free from the mundane and invite the extraordinary into your life, start by opening your mind and heart to the possibilities waiting for you in the cosmos.

Chapter 5: Techniques for Summoning UFOs

5.1 Meditation and Visualization Practices

Exploring meditation techniques can deeply enhance our psychic abilities and strengthen our connection to the universe. I discovered that by focusing on my breath and enabling my mind to settle, I could access deeper states of awareness. One method I found particularly effective is the practice of mindfulness meditation, where I simply observed my thoughts without judgment. This openness creates a space for intuitive insights to surface. As I sat in stillness, I began to sense energies around me, and with consistent practice, my intuition became more pronounced. Bringing in techniques like chanting or visualization during meditation can also amplify this connection. Visualizing light surrounding you while you meditate can act as a magnet for higher vibrational energies, making it easier to tap into psychic phenomena. It's a journey that requires commitment and patience, yet the results can be truly astounding.

Guided visualization exercises specifically designed for summoning UFOs offer an exciting avenue to explore. In one of my experiences, I created a mental framework for this by envisioning a serene, open space under a starlit sky. I would often incorporate elements like the sound of gentle waves and a soft breeze, creating a tranquil setting where I felt connected to the cosmos. As I visualized, I called upon these extraterrestrial beings, inviting their presence into my serene environment. I imagined a beam of light descending from the sky, illuminating the space around me. In this visualization, I found myself open to receiving messages and visuals that went beyond my ordinary perception. With practice, I felt a sense of anticipation and wonder, believing that I was connecting with something greater than myself. The intention behind these exercises is crucial; my commitment to sincerity and curiosity made each session more profound.

5.2 Using Sound Frequencies to Attract

Sound is much more than just vibrations in the air; it is a powerful force that can connect us with higher realms. The universe is filled with vibrations and frequencies, each holding a unique energy signature. This concept first fascinated me when I stumbled upon the works of ancient cultures that revered sound as a means to connect with the cosmic. From the harmonious chants of Tibetan monks to the resonating tones of gongs, each sound can resonate profoundly with the universe. It is like we are tuning into a universal radio frequency, where every sound we produce sends a signal out into the cosmos.

The science behind sound lies in its ability to create resonance. When two objects vibrate in harmony, they activate something larger than themselves. This is true for human intention combined with sound; our thoughts and emotions blend with the frequencies we emit, amplifying their reach into the universe. I've often felt a deep sense of connection whenever I played singing bowls, as the vibrations seem to echo not just in the physical space around me, but also through layers of reality, creating a bridge to other dimensions of existence.

I began my journey of summoning UFOs and connecting with extraterrestrial beings by exploring specific frequencies that are known to attract their attention. One of the most powerful tools I've found is the Solfeggio frequencies, particularly 528 Hz, often called the love frequency. This frequency is believed to promote healing and transformation, allowing us to transcend our earthly concerns and tune into a higher vibration. To practice this, I find a quiet space, sit comfortably, and play a recording of this frequency, closing my eyes and visualizing my intentions.

Another method involves the use of toning and chanting. By creating sustained vowel sounds like "Ah" or "Om," I encompass myself in a bubble of resonance that feels inviting to the unseen. During these sessions, I often focus my intention on the sky, calling for a presence. It might sound simple, but the sincerity of the vibrations, coupled with focused intention, can lead to powerful experiences. Over time, I started noticing flickers of light and unusual formations in the sky. It felt as if I was creating a universal invitation, echoing through the fabric of reality.

For anyone interested in exploring this path, I recommend starting with meditation combined with sound. Choose a frequency that resonates with you, whether it's listening or vocalizing. Taking your time to breathe deeply, allow the sound to envelop you, and focus on the clarity of your intention can truly elevate the experience. With patience and practice, you might very well find that the universe responds to the beautiful vibrations you create.

5.3 Rituals and Sacred Spaces

Rituals are powerful tools that can deepen your connection to the universe and hone your ability to summon UFOs. When I first began exploring this fascinating realm, I realized that intention was crucial. I crafted a ritual that became my anchor, a sacred practice aimed at aligning my energy with the cosmos. I started by selecting a quiet space, away from the distractions of modern life, where I could focus solely on my purpose. Each time I wanted to reach out, I would set the mood with candles and soft music, creating an atmosphere steeped in serenity. The flickering candlelight became a symbol of my intention, illuminating not just my space but also my mind.

As I embarked on these rituals, I made it a point to integrate elements that resonated with me personally – items like crystals that vibrated at frequencies I sought, or natural objects that held emotional significance. Through repetition, these rituals morphed into a sacred language that spoke to both my spirit and the cosmos. Each time I lit the candles and arranged my sacred space, I felt a direct line of communication with extraterrestrial realms becoming clearer. I learned to focus not just on the act of summoning but on embodying the feelings of openness and curiosity that drew me closer to those I hoped to contact.

Environment plays a vital role in any summoning process. I vividly remember one evening, under a blanket of stars, I ventured out to a secluded hillside. This spot was devoid of light pollution and buzzing city sounds, making it the perfect launchpad for my intentions. Sitting there, I found peace washing over me, and I felt a connection to something greater. The cool breeze and the earthy scent of the grass grounded me, drawing my focus inward and outward simultaneously.

With each breath, I could feel the energy shifting around me. It was as if the very fabric of the universe was responding to my call. As I closed my eyes, I envisioned the craft I wished to encounter, imagining the hum of energy and light surrounding it. Every time I engaged in this practice within that sacred environment, I felt a stronger pull toward what I was trying to reach. I learned that the right setting could amplify my energy, making me a clearer vessel for whatever or whoever I was attempting to connect with. Whether it's an open field, a quiet forest, or a beach at sunset, surrounding yourself with nature can enhance your experience and intentions significantly.

Establishing rituals that resonate with your true self and finding the right environment are critical steps for anyone looking to open the door to unexplained phenomena. If you want to enhance your own summoning experiences, consider crafting your unique rituals. Document your feelings and experiences after each session to refine what works best for you. Pay attention to how you feel in different locations and notice which environments elevate your spiritual practice. This reflection will guide you toward creating a personally meaningful path in your journey to reaching the skies.

Chapter 6: Understanding Extraterrestrial Beings

6.1 Types of Beings and Their Intentions

Exploring various types of extraterrestrial beings and their known motivations opens up a fascinating realm of possibilities. Throughout my journey, I've encountered accounts of different beings, each with unique characteristics and backgrounds. Some individuals speak of the tall, luminescent beings often described as Nordics, who appear to possess a benevolent nature and an interest in guiding humanity towards a higher state of consciousness. They seem to embody a deep understanding of spiritual evolution and often are connected to themes of healing and enlightenment. On the other hand, reports of the more mysterious, often feared "Grays" emerge, beings that are typically associated with abduction narratives. Their intentions seem more complex; they might represent a scientific curiosity, conducting experiments rooted in their own survival or understanding of human biology. Then there are the "Reptilians," rumored to be manipulative and controlling, appearing in conspiracy theories as entities that influence human affairs from the shadows. Each of these types provides a fascinating glimpse into what may motivate them—everything from the quest for knowledge and sustainability to, perhaps, a more ego-driven urge for power. The intentions of these beings are often difficult to pin down, which makes intuitive discernment crucial for anyone wishing to engage with them.

Personal insights on discerning intentions through intuition and communication often lead me to reflect on my own experiences. I've learned that establishing a connection with these beings requires a deep sense of openness and trust in one's instincts. Developing this intuitive communication begins by quieting the mind and tuning into the subtle energies around us. When attempting to summon UFOs or connect with these extraterrestrial entities, a clear intention plays a pivotal role. Visualizing what you wish to experience or learn can dramatically affect the outcome. I often found it helpful to engage in meditation, focusing on heart-centered energy to amplify connection. Additionally, paying attention to synchronicities and feelings during these interactions offers clues about the beings' intentions. If an encounter leaves you filled with fear or confusion, it might signify a misalignment in your resonance, while feelings of love, peace, and understanding generally point towards more benevolent interactions. The ability to feel into these interactions can transform your experience, leading to more positive and focused communication.

6.2 The Role of Compassion and Respect

Approaching extraterrestrial contacts with love and understanding is paramount. Each time I think about the possibility of meeting beings from other worlds, I remind myself that these encounters should be grounded in compassion. Love acts as a universal language, transcending barriers that might exist between our species. When I visualize these interactions, I imagine open hearts and kind intentions. This approach paves the way for positive and meaningful exchanges. If we carry fear or skepticism, we only contribute to a divide, one that might keep us away from grasping the wisdom they have to share. It is vital to embrace openness, celebrating the uniqueness of every being we may encounter. We should approach them as potential friends and allies rather than distant mysteries or threats.

Examining the ethical considerations in these unprecedented interactions is crucial. Engaging with other beings doesn't just happen in a void; it requires us to reflect on the implications of our actions. I often ponder questions about their rights, their value, and how our decisions affect the fabric of their existence. Just as we uphold certain morals in our human relations, the same should apply to our dealings with extraterrestrial entities. Respecting their autonomy and recognizing their intelligence are essential pillars that should guide us. In this reflection, I find it necessary to ask, what responsibilities do we carry as explorers? It is not simply about bringing them knowledge but also being mindful of what we share and how we interact. True connection flourishes when we prioritize ethical considerations and respect the lives and experiences of others.

One practical tip I find invaluable is to practice mindfulness and emotional balance regularly. By grounding ourselves emotionally before attempting to reach out to other beings, we foster an environment of peace and receptiveness. This prepares us to be thoughtful ambassadors for humanity, able to engage positively and ethically with whatever we may encounter. The energy we radiate plays a significant role in these interactions, and fostering a loving and respectful presence can make all the difference in how the universe responds.

6.3 Communicating Beyond Words

Exploring non-verbal communication methods with extraterrestrial beings can feel like stepping into a realm where the ordinary laws of interaction don't apply. During my journeys, I've often wondered how truly different our ways of conveying thoughts and feelings could be outside the constraints of Earthly languages. One vivid experience stands out where I found myself in a serene landscape, the air thick with the promise of something extraordinary. Suddenly, I felt a shift—an energy around me that was palpable, yet not visual. It was as if the very atmosphere hummed with a deep understanding. I realized that the beings I sensed were communicating not through spoken words, but through a language of light and emotion. Subtle shifts in color and intensity seemed to convey complex ideas and feelings. It felt like a dance—a mesmerizing exchange that challenged everything I had learned about communication. This telepathic exchange revealed a deeper layer of connection, suggesting that emotions could transcend words, crafting a bond that was both intimate and profound.

Reflecting on my own experiences, I can recall instances where intuitive and emotional exchanges occurred, leaving me with a sense of awe at their purity. One night, while attempting to summon a UFO, I closed my eyes and simply felt. I let go of thoughts and allowed the essence of my spirit to stretch and reach out into the cosmos. There was no need for words; my emotions flowed out, wrapped in intentions of peace and curiosity. In that moment of stillness, I perceived a response—a gentle warmth that enveloped me, as if my thoughts and heart's wishes were heard. The connection was raw, filled with empathy and understanding, creating an emotional bridge where I felt utterly connected to something greater than myself. This experience taught me that sometimes, words are unnecessary. The unspoken bond forged through emotions and intuition can be more powerful than any phrase we might conjure. It beckons us to explore further, to seek out the unseen connections that link all existence.

Opening ourselves to this non-verbal communication invites a deeper engagement with our own intuitive faculties. Embrace moments of stillness and allow your feelings to surface without the barriers of language. Keep your heart open and let your essence expand. Each time you attempt to reach out to extraterrestrial beings, remember that energy and emotion speak volumes, often more so than the human voice ever could. Tuning into this deeper frequency may lead to profound experiences and insights that will reshape your understanding of connection itself.

Chapter 7: The Power of Community

7.1 Finding Like-Minded Individuals

Community support is crucial when embarking on the journey of cosmic exploration. It can feel daunting to venture into the unknown, especially when it comes to the phenomenon of UFOs and the search for extraterrestrial intelligence. Finding others who share your curiosity and enthusiasm makes the journey feel less solitary. Engaging with a community fosters a sense of belonging and shared purpose. Conversations with fellow enthusiasts can inspire new ideas, unveil unique perspectives, and provide the motivation needed to push through doubts and obstacles. Together, we can create a vibrant collective that not only supports our individual quests but also amplifies our understanding and experiences. When we gather in groups, whether online or in person, we become a powerful force, sharing valuable insights and encouraging each other's growth. This unified energy is essential, especially when navigating the complexities of what it means to explore the cosmos.

Reflecting on my own experiences, I remember the first time I attended a local UFO meet-up. I was nervous, unsure of how my interests would be received by others. However, what I discovered was a welcoming environment filled with individuals who were just as intrigued and eager to explore the mysteries of the universe. We bonded over shared stories of sightings and thoughts about ancient astronauts. One individual, in particular, became a close friend. Our countless late-night conversations about theories, documentaries, and possible aliens transformed both my understanding and appreciation of the subject. Each shared experience bolstered our courage to dive deeper into the unknown, and it was through this relationship that I learned to trust my instincts more than I ever had before.

Finding supportive relationships like these not only enhances the journey but also serves as a reminder that we're not alone. The sense of camaraderie eases the anxieties of our pursuits, allowing us to explore additional avenues, such as meditation or astral projection, to summon UFOs or connect with the cosmos. Surrounding yourself with people who share your passion is not just beneficial; it is transformative. Seek out workshops, online forums, or local groups dedicated to UFO research and cosmic exploration. The connections you forge will inspire you and may even lead to extraordinary experiences that change your understanding of the universe.

7.2 Organizing Group Summoning Events

Planning a successful group summoning event requires not just intention but also a blend of practical organization and a pinch of creativity. I've found that setting a specific date and time is essential; having a shared commitment strengthens the energy. Choose a serene location, preferably one where the sky is visible, away from city lights. On the day of the event, get your group together early enough for everyone to settle in and connect. Sharing food or drinks can help everyone relax and bond before the summoning begins. Create a calm atmosphere with soft music or gentle sounds of nature, incorporating elements like candles or crystals to enhance the space. Begin with a short meditation to align everyone's energy, ensuring everyone is on the same wavelength as you focus on the intention of your gathering. Discuss what you hope to achieve, allowing each member to express their feelings and thoughts about UFOs. Make sure to encourage open-mindedness and excitement, as this positive energy can significantly amplify your collective efforts.

When it comes to sharing experiences during group activities, you'd be surprised at the collective energy that can form. During one of my gatherings, I noticed that once we focused our minds on a single intent, something remarkable happened. We all began to feel a heightened sensitivity to the environment—the tiniest sounds turned into a symphony of energy flowing around us. People reported feeling tingles in their fingertips or a warmth spreading through their bodies, all signals that we were truly tapping into something larger. Every voice, every intention seemed to echo in the air, creating a palpable intensity that could almost be seen. Some group members even claimed to have seen lights flickering in the sky moments after our session, which became a moment of shared awe and connection. Those experiences not only deepened our beliefs but brought us closer together as a community seeking truth beyond what we've been taught.

Remember, when you organize these events, it's not just about the outcome but also about the journey of connecting with like-minded individuals. Each session adds layers to your understanding and the collective dreams of the group. Bring a journal to document your experiences, thoughts, and the strange occurrences that might follow your meetings. This way, you can track how energies shift and evolve over time, thus enriching your explorations in the fascinating realm of UFO summoning.

7.3 Shared Experiences: Strength in Unity

There is something incredibly powerful about shared experiences, especially when it comes to summoning. When we gather with others, our collective intentions amplify the energy of our desires, creating a dynamic force that is greater than the sum of its parts. I have felt this firsthand during numerous group gatherings, where the air crackled with a unique energy as we focused on a common goal—connecting with something beyond our understanding. The more people unite in intention, the more the universe responds. It's as if our combined thoughts and emotions form a conduit, channeling our hopes into reality.

One evening stands out vividly. A group of friends and I decided to hold a night of summoning. We drove to a quiet field, far removed from city lights, and sat in a circle under a vast canopy of stars. Each of us shared our own transformative experiences with UFOs, recounting moments of wonder and awe when we felt connected to something greater than ourselves. As we shared, I could feel our energies coming together, creating an invisible thread binding us, and in that moment, I knew we were tapping into something profound. Suddenly, a bright flash zipped across the sky, leaving us breathless, cementing our belief in the collective power of our intentions.

Sometimes, the simplest gatherings can yield the most remarkable results. There was a time when I attended a small community meetup, which turned into an unexpected experience of synchronicity. While discussing our unique paths to understanding the universe, we casually looked up at the sky. To our astonishment, a series of lights danced overhead, almost as if they were responding to our discussion. We didn't plan it; we didn't try to summon anything specific, but our shared joy in exploring the unknown manifested in real-time. This taught me the importance of maintaining an open heart and mind. Whether it's a large gathering or an intimate conversation, the strength found in unity can bring about extraordinary experiences in ways we might never fully understand. Embrace these moments, for they are the whispers of the universe guiding us toward deeper connections.

To enhance your own summoning experiences, consider gathering a small group of like-minded individuals who share your passions and intentions. Create a space where everyone feels safe to express themselves, fostering an environment of openness and unity. Remember that the energy you create together can be a powerful tool. Use meditation, shared intentions, or even a simple circle of storytelling to deepen these connections and amplify your collective frequency.

Ultimately, it's about being present, open, and ready for whatever wonders the universe may bring.

Chapter 8: The Ethics of Contact

8.1 The Responsibility of Knowledge

The discovery of evidence suggesting extraterrestrial existence poses immense ethical implications. As I delve into this uncharted territory, I find myself grappling with the weight of this new understanding. If we are indeed not alone, the knowledge of alien life brings forth questions about our responsibilities as humans. It's crucial to consider how this knowledge impacts our moral duties to one another and to these non-human entities. With great knowledge comes great responsibility, and I often wonder, do we have the right to keep such monumental discoveries to ourselves? Sharing this information can lead to fear or, conversely, inspire hope in a deeper understanding of our place in the universe. The challenge is to navigate this knowledge responsibly, fostering an open dialogue without instilling panic or chaos among those who aren't yet ready to accept this reality.

Reflecting on my personal responsibility in sharing this newfound knowledge has been an introspective journey. I have realized that with every piece of information I encounter about UFOs and extraterrestrials, there's an inherent duty to consider how I disseminate this information. The way I share my insights can influence others' perspectives, potentially shaping the way we collectively approach this subject. Do I present it as factual evidence or mere speculation? Engaging discussions around these topics can lead to a greater sense of unity or divide, depending on how I choose to communicate. I've found that incorporating understanding and an open mind when discussing these matters invites curiosity rather than fear. It allows others to explore the possibilities without feeling overwhelmed. It's not just about sharing what I know; it's about cultivating a space where others feel safe to explore their thoughts and feelings about this vast universe and our connection to it.

Conversations about extraterrestrial existence should not only highlight the discoveries but also evoke a sense of community in this exploration of the unknown. The knowledge we acquire must serve as a tool for building connections rather than erecting walls. I've learned that providing context, encouraging questions, and valuing diverse opinions can enhance the dialogue around this topic. Even more importantly, when I share my experiences in trying to summon UFOs, I do so from a place of excitement and wonder, rather than fear or desperation. By framing my experiences positively, I create an inviting atmosphere, encouraging others to engage with the unknown courageously. Sharing responsibly and mindfully can empower others to step out of their comfort zones and explore the mysteries that lie beyond our earthly existence.

8.2 Intentions and Ethics in Summoning

Understanding how pure intentions can impact the quality of communication with other beings is crucial for anyone interested in summoning UFOs. Over the years, I have observed that when I approach these experiences with a genuine heart, the results are profound. Pure intentions create a positive energy that resonates with the cosmos, allowing for more meaningful interactions with otherworldly beings. This energy shift can enhance clarity in the communication process, fostering trust and connection. I've come to realize that distractions, doubt, or selfish motivations can cloud the channel, leading to chaotic or unsatisfactory exchanges. Therefore, aligning one's thoughts and feelings to a state of purity and openness is essential for successful summoning practices.

Examining personal views on ethics in the UFO community reveals a complex landscape. Some practitioners in this realm adopt a mindset that prioritizes the acquisition of knowledge and experience, often at the expense of ethical considerations. However, I believe that every interaction with these beings carries a responsibility. When I engage in summoning, I see it as a two-way communication where respect, consent, and understanding play pivotal roles. The ethical implications extend beyond mere curiosity; they encompass the wellbeing of all entities involved. Treating these experiences with reverence and accountability not only enriches the exchange but also safeguards my integrity as a summoner. Upholding these ethical standards enhances the trustworthiness of our community and strengthens the bonds we seek with the universe.

A practical tip for anyone looking to summon UFOs effectively is to start with a clear intention, and then create a quiet space to reflect on your motivations. Before each session, I find it helpful to meditate for a short while, focusing on the feelings of peace and goodwill. This creates a conducive atmosphere for interactions, paving the way for authentic communication. Combine this heartfelt clarity with respect for the beings you're attempting to contact, and you're more likely to witness lasting and transformative experiences.

8.3 Navigating Fear and Skepticism

When I first delved into the world of UFO summoning, I quickly encountered a wall of fear and skepticism. The questions and doubts rattled in my mind: What if I attract something dangerous? What if I'm just wasting my time? These fears are common among those exploring the unexplained. I learned that the doubts often stem from societal norms and the ingrained belief that anything beyond our understanding is simply impossible. Conversations about UFOs can quickly turn to ridicule, and this pressure can deter many from sharing their experiences.

However, confronting these fears head-on is crucial. I found it helpful to remind myself that fear often arises from the unknown. By educating myself about the phenomena, I began to unravel the threads of skepticism that haunted me. Researching credible accounts from others who have successfully summoned UFOs emboldened me. I also learned that experiencing fear does not mean you are weak; rather, it is a natural emotion that everyone feels when stepping outside their comfort zone. Recognizing that fear is simply a part of the journey allowed me to push through and embrace the unknown.

As I grew more comfortable, I also had to navigate the negativity that can arise within the community. Some individuals may dismiss your experiences or belittle your efforts, and this can be disheartening. I found that surrounding myself with like-minded people who supported my journey was one of the best coping strategies. Engaging in positive discussions and sharing our experiences fostered a sense of belonging. When negativity crept in, I would practice mindfulness techniques to ground myself, returning my focus to my intentions and experiences. It's important to remember that you are not alone in your pursuits; connecting with others who share your goals can bolster your confidence. If you're feeling overwhelmed, take a step back, breathe deeply, and remind yourself that your journey is valid. Embrace the curiosity and keep pushing through the skepticism, and you might just find the incredible awaiting on the other side.

Chapter 9: Tools for the Journey

9.1 Essential Gear for Stargazers

Stargazing and UFO watching require a blend of curiosity and the right gear to truly enhance your experience under the night sky. While the vast expanse of the universe is captivating on its own, having the proper equipment can elevate your ability to observe and appreciate celestial wonders. A quality pair of binoculars is often my go-to for getting a closer look at the stars, planets, and, yes, any unidentified flying objects that might grace the night. Binoculars offer portability and ease, allowing for spontaneous sessions when the skies clear. I've spotted some intriguing lights soaring across the horizon simply by pulling my trusty binoculars from my backpack.

A telescope is a great next step for those looking to delve deeper into astronomy. While it provides a more detailed view of celestial bodies, it can be somewhat cumbersome to transport. I recommend opting for a telescope that is easy to set up and take down, so you can focus on what really matters—your observation. For those night sessions, a star map or smartphone app can become your best friend. These tools help you identify constellations and locate planets, which can be just as thrilling as waiting for a UFO to zip overhead. If you're serious about UFO watching, consider a night vision device. These can enhance your ability to see in low-light conditions, allowing you to spot those mystery objects even in the darkest hours.

Reflecting on my own experiences, I can't emphasize enough the value of a comfortable blanket or reclining chair for those long nights spent gazing upward. The last thing you want is back pain interrupting your awe as a mysterious orb glides across the sky. I often bring along a thermos filled with a hot drink to keep me cozy and alert during chilly evenings. There have been nights where that warm sip made all the difference in keeping my eyes fixed on the skies when I could have easily given in to the pull of sleep.

When it comes to practical recommendations, I've found that listing down any strange sightings can be quite helpful. Noting the time, date, and description of what you saw can paint a clearer picture of your experiences. You might start to notice patterns in your observations. Plus, sharing your documented encounters with fellow stargazers not only fosters connection but can also provide valuable insights. Always be prepared to be skeptical about your own sightings. A bit of critical thinking can enrich your UFO spotting adventures and help reduce the chance of misidentification. Finally, my greatest tip? Always take your time to simply enjoy the vast mystery of the universe above you. Whether or not you see a UFO, the experience of stargazing has its own undeniable magic that is entirely worth it.

9.2 Tech and Applications for UFO Encounters

In today's digital age, technology has surprisingly begun to bridge the gap between our earthly perceptions and otherworldly possibilities. I've spent countless nights gazing at the stars, fueled by both curiosity and expectation. The advent of smartphones and a plethora of applications have transformed how we explore UFO encounters. These tech innovations make tracking sightings easier and let us document experiences as they happen. For instance, apps like SkyView and Star Walk not only help identify celestial bodies, but they also allow enthusiasts to tag potential UFO sightings, instantly sharing them with a global community eager to decode the mysteries above.

Moreover, many of these applications come equipped with augmented reality features, enhancing our viewing experience and making it more interactive. I have often utilized these tools to pinpoint objects that I initially thought were satellites or planes, only to have them morph into something more unusual before my eyes. The combination of GPS technology and user-generated reports creates a rich tapestry of sighting data, helping all of us understand patterns in UFO activity. This tech empowers individuals like me, making it possible to not just witness something extraordinary but also connect with others who share this fascination.

After spending substantial time experimenting with various apps, there are a couple that have truly stood out. One of my personal favorites is UFO Radar, which utilizes real-time location data to help you discover sightings near you. It's incredibly user-friendly, allowing me to jump directly into viewing what others have reported in real-time, creating a sense of urgency and excitement. The geolocation feature makes it easy to focus not just on UFOs in the night sky, but also to grasp regional trends in sightings.

Another must-have app in my toolbox is MUFON's Sightings. It's not only effective but also one of the easiest to navigate. Every sighting is plotted on a map and detailed with descriptions and images. One night, I discovered a report of a sighting just a few miles away from where I was. It inspired me to take my camera and step outside, fostering an exhilarating adventure that I otherwise might have missed. This app encourages a culture of sharing experiences; it's as if we're all part of one big cosmic family, sharing the thrill of the unknown in real-time. Keeping my eyes on the sky and my phone at the ready has opened a door to possibilities I never dreamed of. If you're serious about UFO encounters, dive into these apps and let them introduce you to a world that waits just above your head.

Knowing how to harness these tools not only enhances your UFO spotting experience but can often lead to more profound insights into the phenomenon. The next time you look up at the night sky, have your app ready to document the unexpected. You never know what might happen when you're prepared.

9.3 Keeping a Journal: Documenting Your Experiences

Maintaining a detailed journal of my experiences has become an essential part of my journey. As I navigated through the complexities of life, particularly while seeking to escape the confines of the matrix, I realized the value of documenting not just the events that transpired, but also my reflections on them. Journaling allows me to capture fleeting thoughts, document unusual encounters, and make sense of my feelings about them. Each entry acts as a snapshot of my state of mind, helping me to piece together patterns, understand my emotional responses, and track my own personal growth over time.

Throughout my journaling journey, I cultivated some techniques that enhance the experience. I often start with a simple date and location, grounding myself in the moment. Then, I write freely, allowing my thoughts to flow without worrying about grammar or structure. This technique lets me capture raw emotions and ideas that may otherwise slip away. I also keep a section dedicated to my dreams and any unusual occurrences, as it seems they often signal deeper insights about my waking life. I use colors and sketches to emphasize specific feelings or vibes, creating a more visceral record of my experiences. I find that writing in a dedicated, inspiring space enhances my connectivity with the universe, making it easier to summon UFOs as my intentions become clearer. One practical tip is to make journaling a daily habit, even if it's just a few sentences; consistency turns it into a cherished ritual that can guide your path into the extraordinary.

Chapter 10: Decoding the Messages from Beyond

10.1 Interpreting Signs and Patterns

Every evening, as twilight sets in and stars begin to twinkle, I prepare myself for a deep dive into the cosmos. I've learned that interpreting signs and patterns during cosmic communication is an art that requires practice and intuition. It's not just about looking up and waiting for a UFO to appear; it's about tuning into the subtleties that the universe offers. Over time, I've developed skills to decode these signs, starting with the simplest movements in the sky to the more complex messages that reach us when we're fully open to receiving them. This involves not only gazing at the stars but also paying attention to my feelings, thoughts, and the synchronicities that unfold in my daily life. The more I practice, the clearer these signs become. Whether it's a distinct change in the atmosphere, a sudden chill, or the formation of clouds that shape unique patterns overhead, each detail holds a potential message. Embracing stillness and mindfulness can amplify our ability to recognize these cosmic whispers, allowing for a more profound connection to the universe.

One of my most memorable experiences occurred during a night vigil, where I sat alone beneath an expansive sky. I was silently searching for answers to pressing questions in my life. As I directed my energy toward the heavens, I noticed a series of shooting stars streaking across my line of sight in rapid succession. At first, I thought they were just coincidental celestial events; however, I began to feel an overwhelming sense of peace wash over me, which was unusual amidst my chaos. I reflected on my life and realized that these shooting stars coincided with my thoughts about letting go of fear. This pattern was unmistakable; the universe was guiding me to trust and embrace change. Another time, while meditating, I saw flashes of light flickering around me; it felt as if the cosmos were responding to my inner dialogue. I recalled how my emotional state at that moment shifted towards gratitude and openness, reinforcing the idea that our energies truly resonate with cosmic frequencies. These experiences taught me that interpreting subtle messages can profoundly impact our paths, encouraging us to align with our true selves in the journey of escaping the matrix.

Embrace the practice of journaling your experiences. By noting the patterns you discern and the feelings you encounter during your cosmic communications, you can create a personal guidebook of your encounters. Over time, this practice may sharpen your sensitivity to signs, revealing deeper insights with each celestial connection.

10.2 Personal Revelations and Guidance

Recognizing personal revelations that accompany contact can be a profound experience. Many of us go through life with our eyes closed, caught up in the daily grind, unaware of the extraordinary opportunities for growth and understanding that are right before us. When contact occurs, it opens a doorway to insights that can radically shift our perspective. These moments can feel like awakenings, illuminating truths we might have otherwise overlooked. I often reflect on how these revelations mold our decisions, relationships, and even our purpose. Each insight builds upon the last, weaving a tapestry of awareness that helps us discern the reality beyond our everyday existence.

One of my most transformative moments occurred unexpectedly. I remember a quiet evening spent in my backyard, looking up at the stars, lost in thought about life and my place in it. Suddenly, I spotted an unusual light darting through the sky. My heart raced, both in fear and excitement. As I focused on the phenomenon, I felt an overwhelming rush of energy coursing through me. In that moment, my mind flooded with clarity about my life's path. It was as if the universe had pulled back a veil. The insight that struck me was simple yet profound: I had been holding back on my true desires for the sake of comfort and conformity. The contact, however brief, was a call to action. I knew I had to change my life dramatically, to step out of the comfort zone I had been so reluctant to leave.

It's vital to remain open to these revelations, as they often come when we least expect them. I've learned that quiet moments of reflection can invite profound insights. Allowing ourselves to be still, to listen, can initiate a conversation with the universe that leads to significant personal growth. Remember that these experiences may vary greatly from person to person, but each carries the potential for transformation. Embrace these moments and trust the guidance that comes. To invite such experiences, set aside time for daily meditation and contemplation, focusing on your intentions. This practice can heighten your awareness and draw remarkable insights into your life.

10.3 Global Messages: What They Mean for Us

Exploring the deeper meanings of events and phenomena often feels like drilling down through layers of stone, with each layer telling a story about what it signifies for humanity. Global messages, whether they come from unexplained occurrences in the skies or the whispers of the universe felt during meditation, suggest that we are all interconnected in a way that transcends time and space. These messages may point us toward a collective awakening, urging us to look beyond the mundane and embrace the extraordinary possibilities that are available to us. Every sighting of an unidentified flying object (UFO) or mystical encounter serves not just as an enigma, but as a call to reevaluate our understanding of existence. Each event can be seen as a nudge from a higher intelligence, inviting us to quest for meaning and connection in a world that often seems disjointed. It's as if the universe is tapping us on the shoulder, saying there's more for us to discover if we only choose to raise our gaze and open our hearts.

Connecting personal stories to the universal themes isn't just about sharing experiences; it's a way to create bridges between individual and collective consciousness. Each tale of a personal encounter with the unknown holds a mirror to the experiences of countless others. I think about the moments when I realized I wasn't alone in my curiosity, when I found others who were similarly intrigued by the great mysteries of life and the cosmos. It's fascinating how a single experience can resonate so broadly, sparking conversations that delve into existential questions of purpose, belonging, and the very nature of reality. We might share our stories of sleepless nights spent searching the skies or the dreams filled with visions of extraterrestrial landscapes, and in these exchanges, we find common threads that unite us. What we experience on an individual level often reflects the broader quests of humanity, a yearning for understanding and a desire to break free from the confines of what we've been taught as 'normal.' By sharing these narratives, we contribute to a shared tapestry of thoughts and feelings, woven together by the threads of our seeking souls.

As we navigate these messages and connections, it helps to ground ourselves in practical exercises that strengthen our ability to reach beyond the ordinary. One powerful technique I've found is to set aside time for contemplation under the stars, allowing my mind to wander and connecting with the vastness above. Simple practices such as journaling about these experiences or invoking intentions before stargazing can heighten our receptivity to any signs or synchronicities that may come our way. Creating a ritual around this can enhance our awareness, helping us to tune into the energies and messages that await our recognition. By being open and attentive, we allow ourselves to not just consume the messages of the universe, but to actively engage with them, transforming our personal narratives into vibrant parts of a much larger story.

Chapter 11: Mastering Your Mind

11.1 Mindfulness and Presence

Mindfulness has become a cornerstone of my life, a practice that helps anchor me in the present. In a world where distractions are constant and the mind races with thoughts of yesterday and tomorrow, cultivating mindfulness offers a sanctuary—a chance to fully immerse myself in the moment. I remember the first time I consciously chose to embrace mindfulness. I sat in a quiet corner of my home, closed my eyes, and focused on my breath. Inhale, exhale. I realized how often I had been on autopilot, going through the motions without truly experiencing life. This simple act opened up a world where everything felt more vivid—colors brighter, sounds more profound, and even my own thoughts became clearer. Through mindfulness, I learned to observe my thoughts without judgment, allowing me to become a witness to my own experience rather than a participant caught in the chaos. Each moment became a new opportunity to explore and understand the world around me, enhancing my awareness of what it means to truly live.

During my journey towards mindfulness, I discovered a few methods that have been instrumental in helping me maintain presence. One technique is grounding. When I feel the weight of the world or my mind begins to swirl with anxiety, I take a moment to connect with my surroundings. I focus on the sensations of my feet on the ground, the texture of the surface beneath me, and the sounds that fill the air. This act of grounding brings me back to the present, as I remember that I am taking in the world, not just observing it. Another method is journaling. Each day, I keep a journal where I jot down thoughts, feelings, and experiences. This practice encourages me to reflect on my day and identify moments where I felt truly present. By writing it down, I solidify those experiences and intentions, reinforcing my commitment to mindfully engage with life. Lastly, I've found that nature has an incredible ability to pull me into the present. Whether it's a stroll through a nearby park or simply sitting outside for a few minutes, the beauty and simplicity of nature reminds me of the importance of being here now. It's essential to find what resonates with you personally, as these methods are simply tools to help you tap into your own sense of presence.

Throughout this exploration, I've learned that mindfulness is not just a state of being; it's a practice that requires dedication and patience. As you traverse this path, consider setting aside time each day to engage in these practices, allowing yourself to awaken to the magic of the now. Awareness paves the way for deeper connections, not only within ourselves but also with the world around us, making every moment an invitation to experience life in its fullest form.

11.2 Overcoming Doubts and Fears

Fear often thrives in the realm of the unknown. It's a natural response that roots itself in our survival instincts. When I began exploring the concept of summoning UFOs and stepping outside the established boundaries of our society, I was overwhelmed by fears that loomed large. What if I was ridiculed? What if nothing happened? These questions plagued me, but I soon realized that these fears were mere shadows cast by my imagination. Addressing them effectively meant diving into this uncertainty headfirst. I started by researching similar experiences shared by others, which allowed me to see the collective fears and how many had triumphed over them. By focusing on the possibility rather than the improbability, I created a platform for growth that pushed me beyond the fears that threatened to hold me back.

Reflecting on my journey, I recall moments of deep skepticism that made me question my path. It wasn't easy to shake off the doubts sprinkled by friends and family, who often didn't understand my passions. I remember staring at the night sky, contemplating whether I would ever spot a

UFO, all while grappling with what I'd tell those who thought I was chasing shadows. But every time skepticism crept in, I found strength in personal anecdotes, both from my own experiences and those of others who shared their stories of contact and connection. Tuning in to this inner strength not only reduced my fears but fostered a profound sense of purpose within me. Embracing uncertainty led to unexpected discoveries that fueled my fascination. I learned that skepticism can coexist with wonder; the key is how you choose to navigate that space.

As you venture into the unknown, whether that be pursuing your interests in UFOs or breaking free from societal norms, remember that fear can sometimes be your greatest teacher. Take small steps and document your journey, noting your feelings and any unusual encounters. This practice not only helps in providing clarity but also serves as a source of motivation when doubts arise. When faced with uncertainty, remind yourself that the biggest breakthroughs often lie just beyond your fears.

11.3 Techniques for Mental Clarity

Finding mental clarity is essential for anyone seeking to explore the mysteries of the universe. Techniques that promote clarity of thought and intention can be transformative. One effective method I've discovered is meditation. I often sit in silence, focusing on my breath, allowing thoughts to drift away. This practice helps quiet the mind, making space for new insights and connections. Visualization is another powerful tool. I like to imagine a beam of light connecting me to the cosmos, guiding my intentions toward specific goals, whether that's summoning a UFO or discovering new truths. Journaling is also incredibly helpful. Writing down my thoughts and feelings not only clears my mind but also helps me track my progress and realizations on this journey.

Experiences underscore the significance of mental clarity in cosmic exploration. Once, while trying to summon a UFO, I realized how essential it was to be free of clutter in my mind. During an evening under the stars, instead of focusing on my worries, I concentrated on what I wanted to experience. I found that when my thoughts were clear and pure, I felt a deeper connection to the universe. In another instance, after a week of consistent meditation, I had a profound encounter that felt guided. The clarity I achieved allowed me to perceive subtle changes in the environment around me, guiding my attention to a craft just as it appeared in the sky. These moments reinforce the idea that when our minds are focused and clear, we can actively participate in the mystery of the cosmos.

Maintaining mental clarity isn't just for those peak experiences; it enhances everyday life as well. A useful tip I can share is to create a simple ritual. Each morning, set aside a few moments to meditate, visualize, or even write in a journal. This daily practice can help anchor your intentions and keep your mind clear, making it easier to invite extraordinary experiences. With consistent effort, these techniques become second nature, paving the way for richer cosmic connections and deeper understanding of our place in the universe.

Chapter 12: Exploring Alternate Realities

12.1 Definitions of Parallel Worlds

The concept of parallel worlds has captivated human imagination for centuries, manifesting in various cultural narratives, folklore, and even scientific theories. In many ancient mythologies, alternate realities are often depicted as realms occupied by gods, spirits, or other beings. For example, the Norse mythology presents a cosmology that includes nine worlds interconnected by the world tree, Yggdrasil, where beings traverse between realms. Similarly, in Eastern philosophies, particularly within Buddhism, the idea of multiple realities is suggested in the notion of samsara and enlightenment, wherein individuals cycle through different planes of existence based on their actions.

Moving from cultural narratives to contemporary theories, quantum physics has introduced the multiverse concept, suggesting the existence of multiple universes that may parallel our own. This scientific perspective, while modern, resonates with ancient beliefs, showing a common thread through time and cultures. Engaging with these diverse interpretations allows us to explore the common human quest for understanding our place in the cosmos, revealing how intricate and layered our perceptions of reality can be.

Reflecting on my own experiences, the idea of parallel worlds often feels deeply relatable. There have been moments in my life where I sensed a reality just beyond the one I inhabit—a feeling of divergence, as if paths could have separated at any moment. These sensations ignite my curiosity about the potential of alternate dimensions, especially when it comes to the unexplained phenomena surrounding UFO sightings. The stories of people encountering UFOs often draw parallels to these alternate realities; they describe experiences that feel out of this world, or conversations that seem like they belong to a different timeline.

Connecting personal insights with broader concepts, I find that the flexibility of reality can manifest in our beliefs and even in the choices we make. The more we open our minds to the numerous possibilities that exist beyond our visible experience, the richer our understanding of existence becomes. To explore this notion further, consider meditative practices that expand your awareness and invite experiences that align with these alternate realms. Engaging with your intuition and imagination might just help you tap into the mysteries of the universe, allowing for a greater connection to the unknown.

12.2 Personal Anecdotes of Parallel Experiences

Throughout my life, I have found myself stumbling into scenarios that felt like they existed in parallel realities. One vivid experience happened during a camping trip in the mountains. I wandered off the beaten path, feeling an intoxicating pull towards the dense trees. As I moved deeper into the forest, the air changed; it grew thicker, almost like stepping into another dimension. The sounds of the outside world faded, replaced by the whispers of the forest that felt almost sentient. I came across a clearing, and in that moment, time seemed to slow. The colors were more vibrant, the sunlight more golden, as if the universe was revealing itself in layers. It was as if I had opened a portal, experiencing a reality where everything was more alive and connected. I understood then that such encounters were not isolated; they echoed a deeper truth about our existence and the possibility of other realms intertwined with ours.

These surreal experiences have been enlightening in more ways than one. Each time I confronted the unknown, I was reminded of the power of intention and belief. During that extraordinary camping trip, I learned not just to be an observer but to be an active participant in creating my reality. The energy I felt was palpable, showing me how focused thoughts could seemingly weave the fabric of our experiences. I grasped the importance of remaining open to the extraordinary, trusting my intuition, and embodying a spirit of adventure. It reinforced the idea that everything is interconnected; our thoughts, feelings, and experiences are threads in a vast tapestry. This newfound understanding ignited a fire within me, pushing me to explore further, seek more, and ultimately, engage with the cosmos in ways I had yet to imagine.

Practical tip: If you wish to summon experiences akin to my encounters, start by immersing yourself in nature or quiet spaces. Set an intention before you go, focusing on openness and curiosity. Allow your mind to relax and your creativity to flow. Remember, the veil between the realities is thin; practice mindfulness and be attuned to the signs around you. Sometimes, magic awaits just beyond the ordinary, nudging you towards a greater understanding of your existence.

12.3 Tapping into Alternate Dimensions

Accessing alternate dimensions has been a transformative journey for me, one filled with intrigue and profound experiences. I have found that the key to opening these gateways lies in spiritual practices that heighten our awareness and connection to the universe. Meditation stands out as one of the most accessible tools. During my sessions, I focus on my breath and visualize light expanding around me. It's almost like I'm peeling back the layers of reality, creating a bridge to other dimensions. The deeper I go, the more I notice the subtle vibrations that hint at other worlds.

Another powerful technique I've utilized is lucid dreaming. By training myself to recognize when I'm dreaming, I can shift the dream narrative and explore alternate realities. In these dreams, it feels like I am not bound by physical laws anymore. This space becomes a playground where I can summon beings and witness landscapes unfathomable in my waking life. It takes practice to become aware within dreams, but the rewards are immeasurable.

Visualization exercises help as well. Imagining portals or doorways during meditative states has led me to places I never thought existed. Those moments where I feel myself step through an ethereal barrier can be exhilarating. Sometimes, it feels like I'm merging with the very fabric of the cosmos. I harness the energy from these experiences by journaling afterward, capturing every detail before it fades away. This enhances my understanding of the visions and our interconnectedness beyond the mundane.

One particular night stands out vividly in my memory. I had conducted a meditation earlier that day focusing on connection with extraterrestrial beings. When I drifted to sleep, I found myself in a shimmering space, surrounded by entities whose energy was palpable. They communicated not through words but through feelings and images. I glimpsed a future where humanity thrived in harmony with nature and technology, and it filled me with hope. The insights left an indelible mark on my soul, shaping my thoughts and actions.

Another experience occurred during a group meditation intended to summon UFOs. As we sat in a circle under the stars, I became acutely aware of a pulsating energy overhead. In that moment, time felt irrelevant, and I lost my sense of self. Suddenly, a bright light appeared on the horizon, darting in patterns that felt almost playful. My heart raced as I realized we had connected with something beyond our earthly realm. That experience taught me the power of collective intention and belief. The interdimensional connections I made that night encouraged me to deepen my practices and seek out similar attempts to engage with the unknown.

Each of these narratives illustrates not only the reality of alternate dimensions but also the insights they can provide. Embracing such experiences can illuminate our paths and guide feelings about existence beyond the confines of the matrix. I find that keeping an open heart and mind is essential. Every practice, every experience is an invitation to break free from limiting beliefs and explore the endless possibilities of consciousness.

To enhance your own exploration, consider setting a clear intention before embarking on these journeys. Intentions serve as powerful magnets, drawing to you experiences and insights aligned with your desires. Whether it's through meditation, lucid dreaming, or group work, clarity in your purpose enhances the experience manifold.

Chapter 13: The Journey of Self-Discovery

13.1 The Importance of Personal Reflection

Deep reflection has always been a crucial part of my journey toward personal growth and understanding. I didn't realize its significance until I found myself lost in the chaos of life, feeling trapped in a routine that suffocated my creativity and authentic self. Reflection became my escape. It was through sitting alone in silence, allowing my thoughts to flow freely, that I uncovered layers of myself I had long ignored. This practice is not merely a passive indulgence; it is an active engagement with who we are and what we desire. In those quiet moments, I would ask myself pressing questions about my motivations, fears, and dreams. This kind of inquiry creates a deeper connection to one's true essence, and with that connection comes clarity. Clarity allows one to navigate life with purpose, making choices aligned with personal values rather than societal expectations. As I delved deeper into these reflections, I began to recognize patterns in my behavior and circumstances. I learned that acknowledging past experiences, no matter how painful, is essential for moving forward. Rather than seeing them as burdens, I began to view them as vital lessons that shaped my perspective. The art of reflection ignited a transformative process within me, revealing a pathway to liberation from the matrix I had unknowingly constructed around my life.

Reflecting on my own journey, several pivotal moments stand out vividly. One was the realization that I had been following a script written by others—parents, society, friends—rather than writing my own story. During one particularly powerful meditation, I envisioned floating above my life, watching as if I were an outsider. This perspective allowed me to see the limitations I had placed on myself. I understood that I had the power to rewrite those narratives. I looked back on times when fear held me back from seizing opportunities, like the time I hesitated to pursue a passion for art because I feared judgment. It was through these reflections that I came to appreciate the importance of self-compassion. Embracing my flaws allowed me to step into my authenticity. Another turning point was when I began seeking knowledge about the universe beyond our earthly experiences, including the mysteries of space and the possibilities of UFOs. Each reflection was a piece of a larger puzzle, revealing truths that were often hidden beneath the surface. These reflections motivated me to step outside comfort zones, challenge beliefs, and explore the cosmos within and beyond. To this day, I continue this practice, finding that the deeper I reflect, the clearer my path becomes. Keeping a journal has proven particularly transformative. It became my sanctuary for thoughts, revelations, and dreams, where each page turned marked growth and understanding in my quest for freedom.

Engaging in personal reflection is a practice I wholeheartedly recommend to anyone eager to break free from societal constraints. Finding a quiet space, whether it's a cozy corner of your home or a serene outdoor location, create ritual moments for introspection. Dedicate time to write or meditate, explore thoughts and feelings deeply. Be gentle with yourself during this process; there are no right or wrong answers, only opportunities to understand yourself better. Trust that as you peel back the layers of your existence, you will uncover insights that are not only enlightening but also empowering, allowing you to summon the courage to live authentically and without fear.

13.2 Uncovering Your Innate Abilities

Each of us carries within us a spark, a unique ability waiting to be acknowledged and nurtured. I found that identifying these innate gifts wasn't always straightforward. It often required stepping back from the noise of everyday life and listening to that quiet voice inside me. I began to pay more attention to what naturally excited me and what felt effortless. Was it a creative ability, an intuitive knack, or a problem-solving skill? By tuning into what I loved and where I thrived, I started to illuminate paths toward mastery in those areas.

Nurturing these gifts was equally crucial. I dedicated time to practice and explore. I read books, attended workshops, and engaged with communities of like-minded souls who believed in the same capabilities I was trying to uncover. It's remarkable how surrounding yourself with encouraging individuals can foster your own growth. I learned that consistency was key. Each day, I carved out a little space to hone my skills, whether through meditation, artistic expression, or simply reflecting on my experiences. The more I engaged with my abilities, the stronger they became, almost as if they were muscles that needed to be exercised.

Investing time in these practices illuminated not just my path toward personal mastery but also reinforced the importance of believing in yourself. The more I engaged with my gifts, the more they flourished. Today, I encourage anyone seeking to escape their personal matrix and tap into their innate abilities to embrace exploration. Trust the process, take those small steps towards what resonates with you, and keep your heart open to the possibilities that lie ahead. Small, consistent efforts will make a profound difference over time, opening realms of potential you never imagined.

13.3 The Path to Authenticity

The journey to living authentically is like navigating through a dense forest where each step brings you closer to the light filtering through the leaves. At times, this path feels overwhelming. For years, I found myself trapped in a cycle of expectations—those imposed by society, by family, and even by my own fears. Realizing that I was merely playing a role in the grand script of life awakened a longing for something deeper, something true to who I really am. This desire pushed me to explore what authenticity means in practical terms. It became essential to sift through the layers of conditioning over time, to separate my genuine desires from those that had been handed to me by others. This exploration felt like a treasure hunt, each insight a shiny piece of gold that helped illuminate my true self.

The path hasn't been without its challenges. I often hit roadblocks, stumbling into the familiar trap of self-doubt. I recall one evening, walking alone under a starlit sky, grappling with the fear of judgment. I faced the harsh whisper that questioned whether my search for authenticity was foolish. In those moments, vulnerability becomes a double-edged sword. Opening up to friends about my quest felt like taking off a protective shell. The fear of rejection loomed large, yet I found solace in shared experiences. I discovered that many were quietly yearning to break free from their own constraints. This commonality transformed personal struggles into powerful connections, enlightening me on my path. I learned to embrace imperfections and to see them as beautiful markers of my authentic journey. Each challenge reinforced my commitment to live a life true to myself.

Chapter 14: The Interconnectedness of All Things

14.1 The Web of Life and Cosmic Consciousness

The interconnected nature of all living beings and the universe is a reality that often goes unnoticed. As I dive deeper into the fabric of existence, I come to realize that every life form, every star, and every grain of sand is tied to one another in a delicate web. My experiences have taught me that this interconnectedness is felt at both a physical and spiritual level. It's in the laughter of a child playing in a park, the rustle of leaves in the wind, and the distant twinkling of stars on a clear night. When I pause to observe these moments, I can feel the pulse of the universe flowing through everything, reminding me that I am not separate but part of an intricate system that includes all life. I've spent evenings under the vast sky, feeling a profound sense of belonging, as if the universe was whispering its secrets directly to my soul. Each encounter and every innocent gaze I share with a creature in nature helps me grasp the reality of our collective existence. When I sit quietly in meditation, I can almost hear the call of my brothers and sisters in this greater network, urging me to awaken to this truth.

Sharing experiences that reflect the unity of life and consciousness reveals incredible possibilities. There was a night when I stepped outside after a long day, yearning for an escape. The stars above shimmered like diamonds against velvet. In that stillness, I thought deeply about the universe, contemplating our shared consciousness. Suddenly, I felt a rush of energy coursing through me, as if a million thoughts and feelings converged into one moment of pure awareness. It was stunning, as if the borders of my individuality dissolved, and I became one with everything around me. In that moment, I realized that we can invoke these experiences by simply tuning into the frequency of love and unity. I began to understand that this wasn't just a personal experience; it is something available to all of us. The universe communicates with us constantly, and acknowledging this connection can be a powerful catalyst. If you ever find yourself yearning for connection, try stepping outside under the stars and embrace the silence. Breathe deeply and allow yourself to feel that you are part of something larger than yourself. Just as I did that night, you may find that the universe is more responsive than you ever imagined, guiding you toward a path of awareness and wonder.

Remember to find moments in your life to pause and reflect on your connection to the universe. Whether it's during a peaceful walk in nature or an engrossing conversation with a friend, embrace the feelings that arise when you recognize your part in this greater web of life. Through these experiences, we can learn to summon our own consciousness and even the unexpected—a shift in perception that may usher in encounters with the extraordinary, perhaps even UFOs. It's essential to approach this journey with an open heart and mind; the universe responds genuinely to our intentions. Let each interaction and each moment of stillness guide you towards a greater understanding of this ineffable connection, encouraging your own experiences of cosmic consciousness.

14.2 Understanding Our Place in the Universe

As I gaze up at the night sky, the vastness of the cosmos becomes a reminder of our smallness. I often reflect on how conscious beings like us exist in the middle of something so immense and unfathomable. It's a humbling experience to realize that our individual lives are but a whisper in the eternal tapestry of the universe. Consciousness gives us a unique role; it allows us to ponder existence, to explore our connection to the stars, and to question what lies beyond our fragile planet. I wonder about our purpose here. Are we merely observers, or do we have a role in shaping the cosmos through our thoughts and actions? Each moment spent in contemplation brings me closer to understanding the significance of consciousness. It feels as if we are on a precipice, just learning to look beyond the matrix that confines our perceptions. This awareness is not just a philosophical quest; it translates into a profound desire to communicate with the wider universe, to connect with other forms of consciousness that may be out there.

My journey toward understanding our cosmic relationship has often been illuminated by personal experiences that seem to draw on the mystical. I recall an evening in the countryside, where the absence of city lights allowed the stars to shine brighter than ever. As I sat in silence, tuning into the rhythm of the universe, I thought about the interconnectedness of all things. In that moment, the stars felt alive, as if they could hear my thoughts. I raised my gaze and whispered my intention to connect with otherworldly beings. Almost as if responding to my plea, a flicker of light zipped across the sky, leaving me awestruck. That experience changed me. It reaffirmed my belief that we are not alone and that the universe listens. Others have shared similar stories, hints of a collective consciousness that binds us to the cosmos and opens portals to realms not confined by space-time.

Understanding our relationship with the universe encourages us to seek further explorations, not just in the literal sense, like looking for UFOs or other life forms, but within ourselves. Engaging in practices like meditation or star-gazing helps align our internal states with the rhythmic dance of the cosmos. This alignment can heighten our intuitive senses, enhancing our abilities to summon and communicate with entities beyond our earthly realm. Each time I set my intention and open myself to this vast universe, I feel more connected to everything around me. It reminds me that we are all part of something greater, and there are ways we can tap into that energy. Embracing this perspective can transform our understanding of existence and empower us to break free from the confines of our daily lives, truly embracing the vastness of the universe.

14.3 Collective Consciousness and Global Change

Collective human thought has an undeniable impact on global events and consciousness. When I think about how shared beliefs and feelings can shape reality, I remember moments when our community came together for a cause. Each of us brought our individual energies, hopes, and intentions, creating a powerful force that moved beyond just a local event. I often wonder how this collective energy resonates with larger patterns in the universe. For instance, during environmental protests, I felt the collective heart of the participants beating as one. Our shared passion seemed to heighten awareness not just among ourselves but also in the wider world. The way we can influence change through intention is remarkable. Ultimately, it leads me to question what else we could influence if we harnessed this collective consciousness, especially in the search for answers beyond our sight, such as summoning the presence of UFOs.

Connecting personal experiences of community events to larger societal shifts reveals a profound truth: our individual stories weave into the fabric of collective consciousness. I recall attending a community gathering where stories of love, loss, and aspiration filled the air. Each narrative added a thread to that shared tapestry, creating an energy bubble of hope and encouragement. It's as if, in those moments, we weren't just sharing our lives; we were merging our personal truths into something greater. As these experiences accumulate, they can spark significant shifts. When people come together with a unified intention, there's a ripple effect that resonates on a global scale. Sometimes I think about how every small gathering, every shared thought, has the potential to influence not just our community but the world. If we remember this connection, we can become deliberate in our collective minds and desires.

To engage in this powerful exchange of thoughts, we need to consciously steer our communal energies. Practicing meditation or group visualization can help align our frequencies, making it easier to tap into that collective consciousness. It's exciting to think that our shared thoughts can attract more than just worldly changes—perhaps we could even draw in the curious attention of UFOs if we generate the right vibration together. Each step we take in understanding our role within the collective reinforces our ability to create a shift in awareness. As we explore what it means to escape the matrix of mundane existence, remember that even the smallest collective effort can lead to extraordinary opportunities for transformation.

Chapter 15: Embracing the Unknown

15.1 Letting Go of Control

Surrendering control is a crucial part of our journey toward discovering truth and forging genuine connections. It's interesting how our lives often become entangled in the need to manage every aspect, to dictate outcomes, and to hold tightly to what we believe we can manipulate. This tight grip often leads to anxiety, and a sense of isolation, making it difficult to connect deeply with both individuals and the universe around us. When I found myself feeling overwhelmed by the chaos of life, I realized that in many cases, letting go of control was necessary for me to experience the fullness of existence. Surrendering did not mean giving up; rather it became a pathway to clarity. I learned to trust the flow of life, which in turn opened doors to experiences that felt almost magical. The truth is, when we relinquish our frantic attempt to control every detail, we often find ourselves more aligned with the reality we seek.

Ultimately, the act of surrendering control translates into a deeper understanding of reality. It teaches us that our power lies not in commanding outcomes but in aligning ourselves with the energies that surround us. When we stop trying to control every moment, we free ourselves to be present, allowing space for truth and profound connections to flourish. As a practical tip, try creating moments each day where you intentionally step back, breathe, and let experiences unfold without your interference. Whether it's engaging with nature, practicing mindfulness, or simply observing your thoughts without judgment, you may discover places of clarity and insight you had not accessed before.

15.2 The Beauty of Uncertainty

Life is full of surprises, and it's in this unpredictability that I've found a kind of beauty that both thrills and inspires me. When I look up at the stars, I am reminded of the vast mysteries of the universe. Who knows what lies beyond what we can see? Each twinkling star might be home to worlds we can only dream of, and somewhere out there, perhaps some conscious beings are looking back at us, wondering the same thing. Embracing this uncertainty has brought a level of excitement to my life that I never expected. Instead of being paralyzed by not knowing what tomorrow holds, I find joy in the possibilities. This embrace of the unknown opens doors to experiences and encounters that we might miss if we stick to a rigid script of expectations. It calls me to be bold and chase my curiosity into the night, where mysteries await and where I feel more connected to the universe.

Facing uncertainty head-on can feel daunting, yet I've learned that it's in these very moments of discomfort that I experience the most growth. Allowing myself to sit with the unknown has taught me resilience and adaptability. Each time I let go of a plan or expectation, I create the space for something truly remarkable to unfold. When I began this journey of seeking to connect with UFOs, I didn't know what to expect. I found myself in situations filled with ambiguity, yet these experiences shaped my understanding of both myself and the universe. I've learned to trust the process, to listen to my intuition, and to cherish the small steps I take. Embracing uncertainty reshapes my perspective, illustrating that every twist and turn can lead to newfound wisdom, allowing me to evolve beyond the confines of my previous self.

As I continue to explore the beauty of uncertainty, I remind myself to lean into the unknown rather than shy away from it. Each encounter, each moment of hesitation, is just another opportunity to grow and learn. This journey is much like calling out to the cosmos, hoping something extraordinary may respond. Remember, the key lies in remaining open to the wonders that uncertainty brings. When you feel the weight of uncertainty, instead of letting it overwhelm you, consider it a canvas for bold strokes of creativity. Allow yourself to explore new paths, to have conversations with the universe, and above all, to stay curious.

15.3 Preparing for Future Encounters

Embracing the possibility of encountering extraterrestrial beings requires a profound shift in mindset. It's not just about believing that they exist; it's about preparing myself mentally and spiritually for such an encounter. Often, our daily lives are filled with distractions and the noise of societal norms, which can make it challenging to even consider the existence of other life forms. However, when I think deeply about the vastness of the universe, it becomes easier to accept that there's more beyond our earthly experiences. I've found that adopting a mindset of curiosity and openness is essential. This mindset involves shedding fears and preconceived notions about what an encounter might be like.

Creating an internal space that welcomes the unknown challenges me to expand my consciousness. Meditation and visualization techniques help me to cultivate this openness. I frequently imagine what it would be like to meet beings from another world. By picturing these interactions, I enable my mind to explore various scenarios, preparing myself for future possibilities. This proactive mental preparation somehow aligns my energy with my intent, making me feel more connected to the universe. I remind myself that these encounters could offer incredible insights and perspectives, enriching my understanding of life itself.

Anticipation is a powerful emotion that can transform the ordinary into the extraordinary. When I nurture a sense of expectation about a potential contact, magic begins to unfold. Every night spent gazing at the stars becomes a moment filled with possibility. Instead of viewing the sky as a distant expanse, I now see it as a tapestry of opportunities. This cultivation of anticipation turns waiting into an adventure rather than a mundane experience. I find myself more motivated to engage with practices like star gazing, using meditation, and even summoning techniques that keep my energy high and my heart open to the cosmos.

Improving my emotional state in this way not only enhances my readiness but deepens the enchantment of any future encounter. Anticipation fuels my creativity and helps me to tune into signs and synchronicities in my daily life. I start to notice things — like unusual lights in the sky or the subtle nudges of intuition guiding my thoughts. All these elements are part of an enhanced experience. By training myself to recognize these moments, I transform simple observations into profound insights, fostering a deeper connection with the universe around me. Preparing for eventual encounters isn't merely about waiting; it's about enhancing every moment leading up to them. To deepen this practice, I encourage keeping a journal, noting your thoughts and experiences related to these encounters; reflection can bring clarity and align your energy even further.

Also by Jessie Contreras

Messages from the Stars: A Guide to Summoning the Galactic Federation
Celestial Awakening: Ascension and the Art of Summoning UFOs
Energy Vortexes: Harnessing Power for UFO Summoning
The Alien Code: Unlocking the Matrix
The Ultimate UFO Summoning Guide:2026 Edition
How To Master The Ancient Art Of Summoning Motherships
The Resonant Universe: Bioelectrical Energy And The Call Of UFOs
UFOs and the Art of Mimicry: The Hidden Intelligence Behind the Disguise

About the Author

Jessie Contreras is a dedicated researcher of unidentified aerial phenomena whose work blends disciplined observation with an interest in how human consciousness shapes extraordinary experiences. Guided by a lifelong fascination with the night sky, he shares his insights through community work, educational content, and continued study. His mission is to explore the phenomenon with clarity, integrity, and an unwavering commitment to understanding what lies beyond the familiar.

About the Publisher

Summon UFOs is a forward-thinking publishing brand dedicated to exploring the intersection of consciousness, extraterrestrial contact, and human potential. Through its works, the brand presents innovative perspectives on UFO phenomena, blending experiential practices, emerging technologies, and esoteric knowledge into a cohesive framework for understanding and initiating contact. Summon UFOs aims to inspire curiosity, expand awareness, and empower individuals to engage with the unknown in a structured, intentional, and transformative way.